SR

COUNTRIES IN OUR WORLD

SUDAN

Ali Brownlie Bojang

W

FRANKLIN WATTS
LONDON•SYDNEY

D1344843

0049804111 1

This edition published in 2013 by
Franklin Watts
338 Euston Road
London NW1 3BH

Franklin Watts Australia
Level 17/207 Kent Street
Sydney NSW 2000

Produced for Franklin Watts by
White-Thomson Publishing Ltd
+44 (0) 845 362 8240
www.wtpub.co.uk

Series consultant: Rob Bowden
Editor: Sonya Newland
Designer: Amy Sparks
Picture researcher: Amy Sparks

A CIP catalogue record for this book is available
from the British Library.

Dewey Classification: 915.1

ISBN 978 1 4451 1903 8

Printed in Malaysia

Franklin Watts is a division of Hachette
Children's Books, an Hachette UK company.

www.hachette.co.uk

Picture Credits
Corbis: Cover (Penny Tweedie), 8 (Michael Freeman),
9 (Michael Freeman), 10 (Michael Freeman), 18
(Khaled ElFiqi/epa), 21 (Michael Freeman), 22 (Zhai
Xi/XinHua/Xinhua Press), 29 (Mohamed Nureldin
Abdalla/Reuters); **Dreamstime:** 7 (David Snyder),
23 (Condortre), 25 (Philip Dhil); **Getty:** 11 (Robert
Caputo/Aurora); **Photoshot:** 12 (World Pictures),
13 (Everett), 16 (WpN), 19 (UPPA), 27 (Xinhua);
UN Photo: 5 (Tim McKulka), 6 (Tim McKulka), 14
(Tim McKulka), 15 (Shereen Zorba), 17 (Fred Noy),
20 (Fred Noy), 24 (Evan Schneider), 26 (David
Manyua), 28 (Tim McKulka).

Contents

Sudan is the third largest country in Africa and one of the poorest in the world. For more than 50 years, the country has suffered from famine and civil wars. On 9 July 2011, South Sudan became independent from Sudan, after a referendum was held.

Where in the world?

Sudan lies in north-east Africa. Although it is mostly landlocked, it has an 853-km border with the Red Sea. This is important for trade, because it means that ships can travel easily between Sudan and countries in the Middle East such as Saudi Arabia. From there, goods can also be transported to rapidly developing countries such as China and India, which need the resources Sudan exports. Sudan is also developing relationships with other African countries, particularly Kenya, partly through trade and partly because of the movement of refugees.

IT'S A FACT!

Sudan's name comes from the Arabic *bilad al-sudan*, which means 'land of the black peoples'.

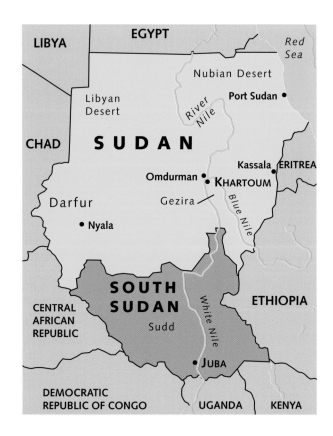

▶ *Sudan has international land borders with South Sudan, Central African Republic, Chad, the Democratic Republic of Congo, Libya, Egypt, Eritrea, Ethiopia, Kenya and Uganda.*

Egyptian and British influences

Since ancient times, the area that is now Sudan has had strong cultural and religious links with its northern neighbour Egypt, and at times the two regions were governed by the same leader. By the middle of the nineteenth century, Egypt had conquered almost all of Sudan, and the Egyptian leaders asked the British to help suppress revolts by the Sudanese people. In 1899, the Egyptians and British agreed to jointly rule Sudan. Until it achieved independence in 1956, Sudan was run as two separate colonies, the south and the north. This separation is thought to be one of the causes of political problems that later followed.

South-North conflict

The people in what was then southern Sudan are mostly Christian or follow traditional beliefs such as animism, where everything in nature is thought to have a soul. The people in modern Sudan (then northern Sudan) are mainly Muslims. When Sudan became independent in 1956, people in the south were concerned that the Muslims in the north would start to control the country. Two civil wars – in which different groups of people within a country fight each other – followed, with devastating consequences. After a referendum in 2011, the people of Sudan voted for southern Sudan to become an independent country called South Sudan.

▼ *A peace march in Juba, the capital of southern Sudan, in 2008. Since this date, these people have gained independence from Sudan.*

The discovery of oil

Oil was discovered in South Sudan (formerly southern Sudan) in the late 1970s. It made some people very wealthy, but these were mainly people who were associated with the government in Khartoum, and foreign oil companies. Ordinary people living in the oil-producing areas have often been moved out of their homes and off their land to make way for the new oilfields. Sudan will now have to learn to live without South Sudan's oil reserves, a source of tension between the two countries.

◀ *This oilfield lies in Bentiu, South Sudan. Since it is largely foreign-owned, most of the profit made from extracting and exporting the oil leaves the country.*

Darfur

In 2003, fighting began in a region of Sudan known as Darfur. This is a very large area – about the size of France. People were angry that the government had done nothing to help them become less poor. During the fighting, thousands of civilians were killed or made homeless following attacks on villages. These attacks were often carried out by groups of men on horseback known as the *Janjawid*, who were supported by the government. It is estimated that the conflict has forced 2 million people to leave their homes and that between 200,000 and 400,000 people have died. This huge movement of people has caused instability in neighbouring regions.

What does the world think?

Sudan is one of the most troubled countries in the world. The USA, the European Union and the African Union have all put pressure on the Sudanese government to end the attacks in Darfur. They are particularly concerned that so many civilians have suffered. The United Nations claimed that the Sudanese government may have committed crimes against humanity and war crimes by its actions in Darfur, and ordered that the president of Sudan, Omar al-Bashir, be arrested and put on trial at the International Criminal Court. However, it is unlikely that this will happen because there may not be enough evidence against him.

▲ *A woman who has been forced from her home by the fighting sits with her child in a makeshift tent in a camp in eastern Darfur.*

BASIC DATA
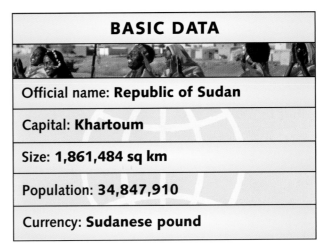
Official name: **Republic of Sudan**
Capital: **Khartoum**
Size: **1,861,484 sq km**
Population: **34,847,910**
Currency: **Sudanese pound**

Landscapes and environment

Sudan is the sixteenth largest country in the world and the third largest on the African continent. It is slightly less than one-fifth of the size of the USA. The landscape is mostly flat and featureless, with desert dominating the north of the country.

The shape of the land

The dominant landscape is desert but there is the fertile valley of the River Nile, which flows through the country from south to north. The highest point in the country is the Deriba Caldera, at 3,042 m, part of the Jabal Marra mountain range in Darfur, that stretches for 60 km.

▼ *In the north sandstorms, known as* haboob, *can completely block out the Sun.*

The dry north

The north is very hot and dry, and temperatures can reach 48°C. The deserts here stretch across Egypt and Libya. Very few people live in this harsh region, but those that do are mainly nomadic tribes who travel around with their herds of goats and camels. There is a short rainy season from July to September, but in some places it does not rain at all.

PLACE IN THE WORLD

Total area: **1,861,484 sq km**

Percentage of world land area: **1.2%**

World ranking: **16th**

Tropical South Sudan

South Sudan was until 2011 part of Sudan, and it is quite different in its geography. It has a hot climate but it has far more rainfall than Sudan. As a result, the landscape in this part of the country is made up of rainforests and swamps.

The southern region

Most of the area is open grassland. This land is ideal for farming as there is enough water. Here most of Sudan's food for export and local consumption is grown, although the main crop is cotton, grown in schemes like Gezira (see below).

GLOBAL LEADER

Irrigation

South of Khartoum, between the White Nile and the Blue Nile, lies one of the largest irrigation projects in the world – the Gezira. Small farms, known as *feddans*, are supplied with water from the River Nile through a series of ditches that total 4,300 km in length.

▼ *Women trample down a mound of cotton at harvest time in the Gezira scheme.*

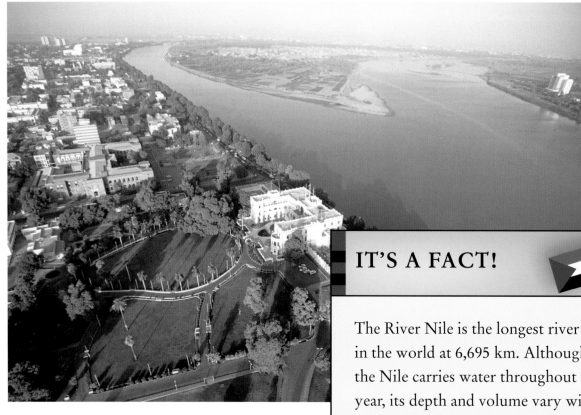

▲ *From the air it is easy to see the point at which the Blue and White Niles meet, with strips of fertile land on either bank.*

The River Nile

The River Nile is often called the 'life-blood' of Sudan. The two Niles, the Blue and the White, meet at Khartoum and flow northwards towards Egypt in a large, S-shaped curve known as the Great Bend. The Sudanese people rely on the Nile for most of their water needs, from drinking water to irrigating crops for food. Two thousand years ago, the Nubian Empire developed along the banks of the Nile in what are now Egypt and Sudan, because the river meant people could grow crops.

IT'S A FACT!

The River Nile is the longest river in the world at 6,695 km. Although the Nile carries water throughout the year, its depth and volume vary with the season, and during droughts the Blue Nile can actually dry up. The White Nile is made up of many small tributaries, but about 94 per cent of its waters are lost to evaporation before it meets the Blue Nile in Khartoum.

Threatened wildlife

Due to hundreds of years of livestock grazing, large areas of Sudan's natural plants have disappeared. Many mammals and birds are endangered, including the Tora hartebeest and the Sahara oryx. One animal that can cope with the harsh desert conditions is the African wild ass, from which the donkey is descended.

Environmental threats

Both Sudan and South Sudan have many environmental problems. In Sudan the deserts are advancing to the north. People continue to cut down trees and overgraze the land, making this problem even worse. In South Sudan, the development of the oil industry has been responsible for damaging the habitats of some animals and has led to a decline in their numbers. Oil pollution and the building of roads and pipelines have also led to a loss of fertile land.

GLOBAL LEADER

The Sudd, South Sudan

The Sudd is the largest area of wetland, or swamp, in the world. It occurs where the White Nile spreads out into an almost completely flat plain. It acts like a giant sponge, holding on to the waters of the White Nile and releasing them slowly throughout the year.

▼ *In the rainy season, the Sudd can increase to the size of England.*

Population and migration

Sudan used to have many more ethnic groups in its population when South Sudan was still part of the nation. Today it is approximately 70 per cent Sudanese Arab, with the rest comprising Fur, Beja, Nuba and Fallata peoples.

PLACE IN THE WORLD

Population: **34,847,910**

Percentage of world total: **0.4%**

World ranking: **35th**

Settlement in Sudan

Over the centuries, people from other African countries have settled in Sudan. Many of these have strong links with other countries in North Africa and the Middle East, and are mainly Muslim. In South Sudan, until recently part of Sudan, most people share their origins with people in East Africa and, in some cases, West Africa.

Quality of life

Most people in Sudan are very poor. Over half the population lives on the equivalent of less than US$1 a day. Poverty causes much ill health. The number of children that die before they are five years old is 86 for every 1,000 births. This compares with five per 1,000 births in the United Kingdom and eight for every 1,000 in the United States.

▼ *A mosque in Kassala, north-eastern Sudan. Most Sudanese follow the Islamic religion but there is a small Christian minority.*

Ethnic groups

Historically, the largest non-Arabic ethnic groups in Sudan were the Dinka and Nuer groups, who live in what is now South Sudan. These groups are made up of many different tribes and do not have a single leader, but share similar traditions and beliefs. Both the Dinka and Nuer rely on raising cattle, often moving around to find the best land for grazing.

Many Nuer and Dinka left the former Sudan because of the civil wars. Some moved to other African countries, but the USA and Australia are also now home to thousands of Nuer and Dinka people. Since South Sudan gained independence, some have been returning to help build up the country.

FAMOUS SUDANESE

Alek Wek (b. 1977)

Alek Wek was born in what is now South Sudan. In 1991 her family fled to the UK to escape the civil war. In 1995 she was spotted by a models' scout in London and she is now a top model.

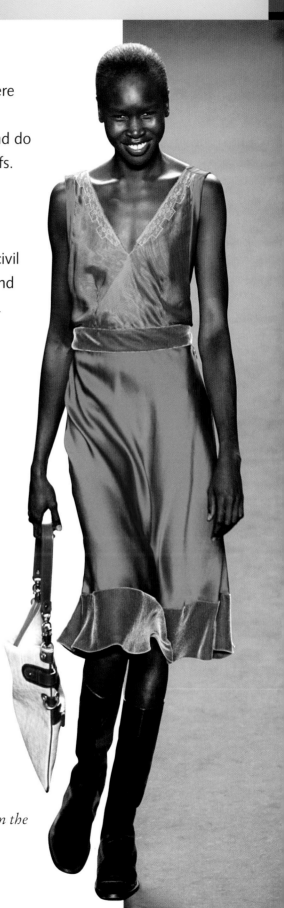

▶ *Alek Wek is from the Dinka tribe, from the area that is now South Sudan.*

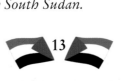

Refugees and internally displaced people

Since fighting broke out in Darfur in 2003, nearly two million people have left the area. Most of them settled in refugee camps, where they lived in makeshift shelters and relied on foreign aid for food and medical supplies. Some people travelled to towns and cities such as Khartoum, or even went to other countries in search of work. It was usually men who went, leaving the women behind.

◀ *These women were forced to flee because of fighting and had to rely on food rations from international organizations.*

GOING GLOBAL

Sudan is badly affected by the emigration of skilled people, mostly doctors and other health professionals. It is estimated that out of 1,500 doctors who graduate each year, 800 leave the country to seek better opportunities in the UK and Ireland, as well as in Saudi Arabia and other Gulf countries.

Fleeing to Sudan

As the same time as people were leaving Sudan, refugees fled to Sudan from conflicts in neighbouring countries, such as Eritrea, Ethiopia, Chad, Uganda and the Democratic Republic of Congo. Because the situation in Sudan is already very difficult, it is extremely difficult to provide help for all these people. The refugee crisis adds to the instability of the region.

▲ *A peacekeeping soldier from the joint United Nations-African Union mission speaks with villagers in the war-torn region of Darfur.*

Peacekeeping and aid

The African Union (AU) is an organization of African countries set up to help one another in areas such as economic development and peacekeeping in troubled regions. As part of the AU, countries including Rwanda, Nigeria and the Gambia have sent peacekeeping forces to Sudan. In 2007, the United Nations took command of the Darfur peacekeeping operation from the African Union.

Humanitarian aid has been sent to Darfur from all over the world. It continues to be very difficult for aid workers to travel around the Darfur region though because of the danger of being attacked by rebel groups. The World Food Programme has provided an air service for foreign aid workers, flying them around the region, which is safer than travelling overland.

Culture and lifestyles

Sudanese culture mixes the traditions and beliefs of all the many tribes that inhabit the country. These varied influences show in the religions, music and fashions of the people in different parts of this large country.

Religion

Religion is a very important part of Sudanese people's lives. Most people in modern Sudan are Muslim, although a few are Christian. Christianity was introduced in Sudan by missionaries in the nineteenth century. They had more success in converting people in the area that is now South Sudan. Many others follow traditional beliefs such as animism, where they believe that everything, including plants and rocks, has a soul. They often hold these beliefs alongside their Muslim or Christian beliefs.

IT STARTED HERE

Whirling dervishes

Sudan's 'whirling dervishes' are known in many countries. They come from a particular Islamic sect called Sufism, which began in Sudan. The dervishes perform a rhythmic dance – accompanied by drumming, twirling round and round, all the time getting faster – which they believe brings them closer to God.

The *souk*

At the heart of every Sudanese town is the *souk,* or market. These are lively, noisy places where craftspeople make and sell glass beads, wood carvings, leather bags and saddles for horses and camels. Food and other household goods are also available to buy at the souks.

▶ *Some people became Christians as a result of European missionaries travelling to Sudan. These boys are receiving religious instruction at a Catholic mission.*

▲ *Football is very popular in Sudan. All over the country, people will get together for a game.*

FAMOUS SUDANESE

Manute Bol (1962-2010)

Manute Bol, born in what is now South Sudan, became the tallest man ever to play in America's National Basketball Association (NBA) league, in 1985. He originally wanted to play football but he soon realized that at 2.31 m (7 ft 7 in) he was too tall, so he turned to basketball.

Sport

Many sports are played in Sudan, including traditional wrestling and horse racing, and at the 2008 Beijing Olympics Sudan won its first-ever medal – silver in the men's 800 metres. Football is the most popular sport, however, and is played all over the country. The Sudanese national football team is nicknamed *Sokoor Al-Jedian*, or Desert Hawks. Even in remote villages children get together for a game. Fans support their favourite teams, but they also keenly follow the leagues in England, Spain and Italy.

Family life

As in many Arab and African societies, the family is very important and highly valued. Families are usually large, and often grandparents, aunts, uncles and cousins all live together. The most important person in the family is usually the oldest man, but sometimes it may be the oldest woman. The Sudanese have traditional views about the different roles of men and women. Women are expected to look after the home and the children, and do not often go out to work.

Hospitality

Sudanese people put great value on welcoming people into their homes, whether they are friends or strangers. Food and drink are served and the guest is very well looked after. A sheep may be slaughtered (killed) for dinner for important guests. Meals are usually eaten from a large communal bowl using the right hand, a spoon or a piece of bread. The Sudanese have a very special way of preparing coffee, where they fry the beans and grind them up with spices.

▼ *Sudanese people believe that cooking and looking after the children are the women's responsibilities.*

Education

School is free and compulsory between the ages of six and 14, but many children in the countryside find it difficult to go to school. Their schools may have been bombed, they may not be able to afford to buy books and uniforms, or they may need to stay at home to work. During the civil war, only one per cent of girls completed their primary-school education. Many schools in Darfur have been destroyed during the conflict.

 Although all children are supposed to attend school until they are 14, war has prevented many of them from keeping up with their education. Adult literacy stands at 61 per cent.

IT'S A FACT!

As many as 70 per cent of the population of Sudan has access to a mobile phone, a much higher percentage than in neighbouring countries such as Ethiopia or Chad. Internet use is also increasing in Sudan at a fast rate.

Music

Many different kinds of music are popular in Sudan, although the strongly Islamic government does not approve of modern music. Some musicians have even been imprisoned; others have left Sudan so that they can play their music freely. This has helped spread Sudanese music around the world.

Economy and trade

In the past, farming was the way that most Sudanese people earned a living. Since South Sudan became independent, oil earnings provide much less income to Sudan. Sudan's government is looking for new income sources.

GLOBAL LEADER

Gum arabic
Sudan is the world's largest producer of gum arabic, the dried-up sap from the acacia tree. It is used in many food products, as well as in lipstick and chewing gum. Almost all Sudanese gum arabic is exported to the USA.

Livestock and crop farming

The type of farming people do depends on where they live. In the north, people look after herds of animals, moving from place to place to find the best land for grazing.

Along the River Nile, it is possible for farmers to grow crops. Pumps and irrigation ditches bring water from the river to support crops such as sorghum, millet and cereal grains.

▼ *A farmer in Nyala harvests the cereal crop sorghum. He was given the seeds by the Food and Agriculture Organization of the United Nations, as part of an international programme to help farmers.*

GOING GLOBAL

Sudan's major trading partners include the United Arab Emirates (63.2 per cent), Saudi Arabia (9.2 per cent) and Ethiopia (5.3 per cent) according to data collected in 2012. Its most important import partners are Macau (part of China), India, Saudi Arabia, Egypt and United Arab Emirates.

▶ *These workers are loading sacks of sesame on to a freighter ship, for export to countries such as China and Egypt.*

Producing to export

Sudan produces many crops for exporting to other countries, but the main one is cotton. There are several fair-trade cotton projects in Sudan, where workers are given a fair wage and where some of the money earned by selling the cotton is invested in the community – for example, in healthcare or schools. Fair-trade goods are very popular in other countries. Sudan is Africa's third largest producer of sugar, after South Africa and Egypt. Sudan also exports sesame, groundnuts (peanuts), gum arabic and livestock, as well as natural gas, gold, silver and many other mineral resources.

Oil – and gold

Oil was discovered in Sudan in the 1970s in the region that is now South Sudan. Several foreign companies were interested in working in Sudan to exploit the oil, but were forced to abandon their plans because of the wars. Oil did become one of Sudan's main exports but most of that revenue now goes to South Sudan. The income from oil helped Sudan's economy to grow but now the government is seeking other sources of revenue. One of these is gold and in 2012, President Omar al-Bashir of Sudan opened the country's first gold refinery. This should help Sudan to make money from gold ore.

▲ *This Chinese farmer is showing a Sudanese man how to sort cucumbers at a Chinese-run farm near Khartoum.*

GOING GLOBAL

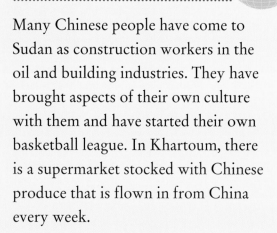

Many Chinese people have come to Sudan as construction workers in the oil and building industries. They have brought aspects of their own culture with them and have started their own basketball league. In Khartoum, there is a supermarket stocked with Chinese produce that is flown in from China every week.

China's special role

China's economy is growing so rapidly that it needs raw materials for its factories and food for its booming population. It has developed strong relationships with many African countries that produce oil, minerals and food products, in order to meet these needs. Sudan is an important provider of raw materials for China. China is particularly interested in oil produced in South Sudan's oil fields. It has built a pipeline from the oil fields to Port Sudan and a tanker terminal at the port. China has tried to resolve conflicts between South Sudan and Sudan regarding use of these shared oil pipelines.

Khartoum develops

In contrast to much of the rest of the country, Khartoum has experienced something of a building boom. During the boom years, up until 2011, the oil industry attracted many foreign businesses, and since 2000, new factories, shopping malls, hotels and office blocks were built, as well as a new airport. The condition of the existing roads improved, and more were built. There are far more cars now than there were just a few years ago.

▼ *Modern hotels were built in Khartoum when the oil industry was booming.*

IT'S A FACT!

During the boom years, Sudan was the seventeenth fastest growing economy in the world, growing at a far faster rate than most industrialized countries. However this was largely because of its oil exports. Now it has a minus growth rate and is ranked 216th in the world for growth. It also has very high levels of inflation.

Poverty in the countryside

The boom in Khartoum did little to spread any wealth to the people living in the countryside. It is estimated that four in every ten children under the age of five are underweight, and most villages still lack roads, electricity and proper drainage facilities. Many people in rural areas still have to walk long distances to draw water from wells.

Sudan is an independent Islamic republic. The country is governed by a small group of Muslim clerics or brotherhoods based in the capital, Khartoum. However, large parts of the country are beyond the control of the government.

The government

In 1989, Omar Hassan al-Bashir overthrew the Sudanese government, backed by the military. In 1993 he became president of Sudan. Until that time, the different regions of Sudan had enjoyed some level of self-government, but al-Bashir took away that power and put it all in the hands of a central government in Khartoum. He introduced Islamic law, known as *Sharia,* throughout the whole country, even for people who were not Muslims. No one was allowed to oppose the government – those that did were sent to prison. Newspapers were not allowed to print what they wanted.

◀ *President al-Bashir (right) meets with the Secretary-General of the United Nations, Ban Ki-moon in 2007 to discuss the crisis in Sudan.*

▲ *Thousands of Sudanese gathered to celebrate the opening of the Merowe Dam, on the Nile near Khartoum, in March 2009.*

Sudan and its neighbours

The introduction of *Sharia* law in Sudan caused concern for some of the country's neighbours. They were afraid that it would spread into their own countries. In the 1990s, Uganda, Kenya and Ethiopia joined together to try and stop the spread of *Sharia* law, and they were supported by the USA. Relationships between Sudan and these countries have been poor ever since, and they have accused each other of supporting rebel groups in each other's countries.

The Nile Basin Initiative

Sudan has better relationships with its neighbours over the River Nile. Although there are sometimes disagreements, the countries work together to make sure they can all benefit from the Nile's waters. The Nile is vital to all the countries through which it passes, and an estimated 300 million people depend on it for domestic water supplies (for washing and drinking) as well as for irrigating crops. These countries have formed an agreement, called the Nile Basin Initiative. Egypt, down-river from Sudan, has helped Sudan with dam-building projects and invested money in a canal-building project in the south to regulate the flow of water.

A terrorist state?

Since 1993, the USA has considered Sudan to be a country that supports terrorism. The US government said that American companies were not allowed to do any business in Sudan. In 1998, it bombed a pharmaceutical factory in Khartoum because it was believed that chemical weapons were being produced there that might be used for terrorist activities. In 2001, the USA started to allow its companies to do business in Sudan once more, because it could not prove that the Sudanese were involved in terrorism.

▼ *These Nigerian soldiers are part of the United Nations-African Union Mission (UNAMID) in Sudan.*

GOING GLOBAL

On 17 November 2006, former UN Secretary-General Kofi Annan announced that Sudan had agreed to allow the establishment of a joint African Union and United Nations peacekeeping force within its borders. This co-operation with an international organization was seen as a sign of Sudan's improved status in world affairs.

A new peace

In 2005, the north and south of Sudan reached a peace agreement. In this agreement, oil deposits were to be shared equally between the north and the south. Although still part of Sudan, the south was allowed to have some control over its own affairs. The results of the referendum held in January 2011 were decisive. South Sudan split from Sudan and became an independent country in July 2011.

▼ *Sudanese people gather to protest against the arrest warrant issued for President al-Bashir.*

Holding Sudan to account

In December 2006, the International Criminal Court decided to bring a case against members of the Sudanese government. It believed some people had committed war crimes and had violated human rights in Darfur. In July 2008, President al-Bashir was charged with genocide for planning to kill all the people of Darfur's three main ethnic tribes, the Fur, the Masalit and the Zaghawa. Although the Court issued a warrant for his arrest, he has not yet been put on trial. In July 2010, the ICC issued a second arrest warrant for President al-Bashir.

When Sudan split into two countries in July 2011, it left some border disagreements and disputes over oil revenues as outstanding areas of tension between the two countries. It needs to overcome these in order to prevent the outbreak of violence. It also needs to resolve the continuing conflict in the Darfur region of the country, to the west.

Sharing the wealth

Sudan is a predominantly poor country, but there are some extremely wealthy people. Oil revenues made some people very rich during the oil boom years. Gold mining and other industries also make a small number of people very wealthy whilst most workers earn below the poverty line. Sudan's government needs to find ways to help the majority of its population rise out of poverty or there may be further unrest and wars in the future.

▼ These children are searching a rubbish dump for food and clothing If life is to improve for the Sudanese people, the country's wealth must be shared more equally.

◀ *Modern cars and Western-style advertising on the streets of Khartoum are signs of Sudan's improved economy.*

Tourism in Sudan

The government knows that it has to find a replacement for the oil income that it depended on so heavily. To balance the books, it has had to introduce big budget cuts, but it is also developing the gold and sugar industries. If peace could be established in Darfur and elsewhere, and if the government developed better roads and transport, tourism could play an important part in Sudan's future. It is an ancient country with a fascinating history, and there are many places of interest that would attract visitors if they felt it was safe to travel there.

Economic prospects

Sudan could be a successful and prosperous nation. It has plenty of land available to grow crops, and enough water from the Nile to irrigate them. This means it could grow enough food for its population as well as for export to other countries, which would bring in much-needed money. For this to happen the government needs to invest in the farming industry, for example by setting up more irrigation projects. This would be a major step in helping the country towards a more stable future, where people in all parts of Sudan may enjoy an improved quality of life.

Glossary

Arab someone who belongs to a race of people that originated in the Arabian Peninsula. Arabs are usually Muslims and speak Arabic.

animism the belief that spirits inhabit all natural objects such as rocks and trees.

civil war a war in which different groups within the same country or region fight each other.

colony a country or a region that is under the political control of another country.

continent one of the world's seven great land masses: Africa, Antarctica, Asia, Australia, Europe, North America and South America.

drought a prolonged period without rainfall.

economy the financial system of a country or region, including how much money is made from the production and sale of goods and services.

ethnic relating to a specific group of people with the same background.

export to send or transport products or materials abroad for sale or trade.

famine a serious shortage of food.

genocide the systematic killing of a group of people, often because of their racial or cultural background.

humanitarian the importance of promoting the welfare of people.

human rights the basic freedoms to which everyone in the world is entitled according to the United Nations Universal Declaration of Human Rights (UDHR).

International Criminal Court an international law court set up in 2002 as the world's first permanent war-crimes court.

irrigation supplying dry land with water by means of ditches and channels in order to make it suitable for growing crops.

nomad someone who has no permanent home and who moves from place to place, often with livestock.

refugee someone who has to flee from their home to another country because of war or persecution.

republic a political system in which the head of state is an elected president rather than a king or queen.

resources things that are available to use, often to help develop a country's industry and economy. Resources could be minerals, workers (labour) or water.

terrorist a person who uses violence or causes fear to try and change a political system or policy.

tributaries a smaller river or stream that flows into a larger river.

Further information

Books

Sudan, South Sudan and Darfur by
Andrew S Natsios
(Oxford University Press, USA, 2012)

Websites

www.bbc.co.uk/news/world-africa-14094995
The BBC's country profile page with facts and all the
latest news about what is happening in Sudan.

www.cia.gov/library/publications/
the-world-factbook/
The CIA World Factbook site. Search the site for
detailed information about Sudan and South Sudan.
Packed with up-to-date information and statistics.

*Every effort has been made by the publisher to ensure
that these websites contain no inappropriate or offensive
material. However, because of the nature of the Internet,
it is impossible to guarantee that the contents of these sites
will not be altered. We strongly advise that Internet access
is supervised by a responsible adult.*

Index

Numbers in **bold** indicate pictures